D0926729

SPOTS OF LIGHT

A Book About Stars

by Dana Meachen Rau   illustrated by Denise Shea

PICTURE WINDOW BOOKS
Minneapolis, Minnesota

Thanks to our advisers for their expertise, research, and advice:

Dr. Stanley P. Jones, Assistant Director
NASA-sponsored Classroom of the Future Program

Susan Kesselring, M.A., Literacy Educator
Rosemount–Apple Valley–Eagan (Minnesota) School District

Editorial Director: Carol Jones
Creative Director: Keith Griffin
Editor: Christianne Jones
Story Consultant: Terry Flaherty
Designer: Joe Anderson
Page Production: Picture Window Books
The illustrations in this book were created digitally.

Picture Window Books
5115 Excelsior Boulevard
Suite 232
Minneapolis, MN 55416
877-845-8392
www.picturewindowbooks.com

Printed in the United States of America.

Library of Congress Cataloging-in-Publication Data
Rau, Dana Meachen, 1971-
Spots of light : a book about stars / by Dana Meachen Rau ; illustrated by Denise Shea.
p. cm. — (Amazing science)
Includes bibliographical references and index.
ISBN 1-4048-1139-7 (hardcover)
1. Stars—Juvenile literature. 2. Constellations—Juvenile literature. I. Shea, Denise, ill.
II. Title. III. Series.

QB801.7.R38 2006
523.8—dc22   2005003730

Table of Contents

Bright Lights

Twinkle, twinkle. The night sky is filled with thousands of lights. These lights are stars. What do stars look like to you? Fireflies? Glitter? Shiny coins? Look into the sky and think about these little dots of light.

Have you ever drawn a star? Your star probably has five points. Real stars aren't pointy. They are round.

FUN FACT

Stars look tiny from Earth. However, most stars are much bigger than Earth. They look small because they are so far away.

Energy

Our bodies use energy every day. Energy helps you run a race or do homework. Stars use energy, too. They give off two kinds of energy—light and heat.

FUN FACT

Stars are balls of hot gas. The inside of a star
is its hottest part. The inside of a star is
60,000 times hotter than the hottest oven.

Birth of a Star

How are stars made? There are clouds of gas and dust in space. When gases clump together, they get hotter and hotter. A star is born.

Eventually, a star runs out of energy and dies. Some dying stars explode. An exploding star is called a supernova. It looks like fireworks.

FUN FACT

Not all dying stars explode. Some just get cooler and smaller until they disappear.

Everybody's Different

Look at your friends. Does everyone look the same?

Just like your friends, each star is different. Some stars are small. They are called dwarf stars. These stars are usually dim. Some stars are large. They are called giants. Larger stars are usually bright.

FUN FACT

Some stars are even larger than giant stars. They are called supergiants.

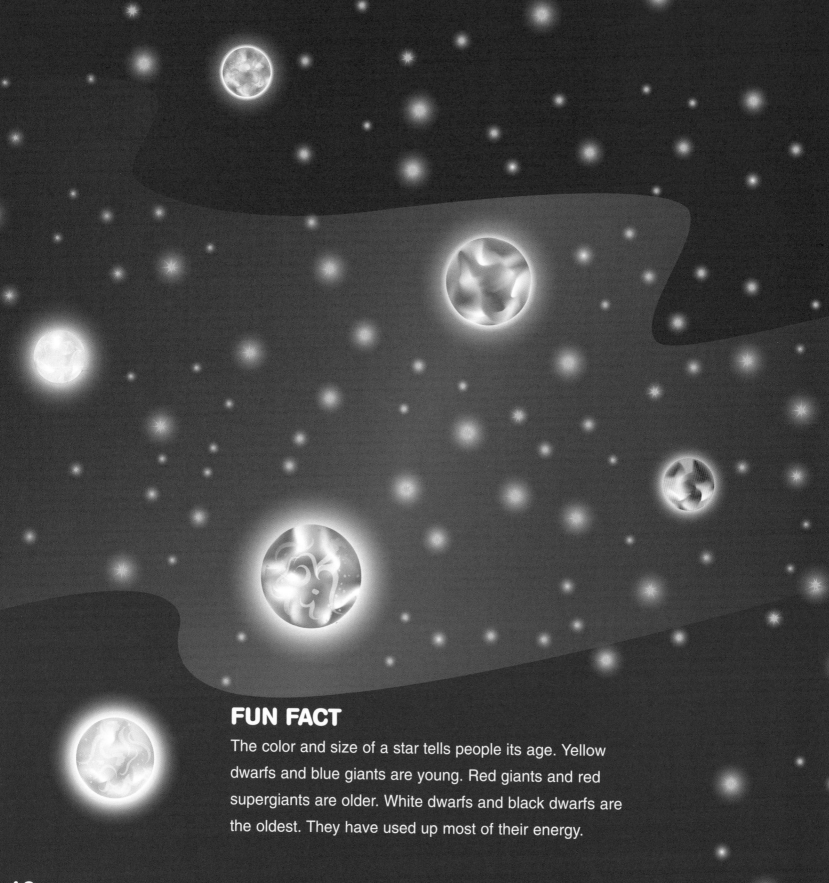

FUN FACT

The color and size of a star tells people its age. Yellow dwarfs and blue giants are young. Red giants and red supergiants are older. White dwarfs and black dwarfs are the oldest. They have used up most of their energy.

Star Colors

Stars are different colors. Some are white, some are black, and some are brown. Some are blue, some are yellow, and some are red.

Blue stars are the hottest stars. Red stars are the coolest. Yellow stars are in between.

Our Star

Not all stars are tiny dots at night. You can see one star during the day. It is our sun.

The sun is a yellow, middle-sized star. It looks big because it is the closest star to Earth. Even on cloudy days, the sun is still shining.

FUN FACT

Most stars are far away, so we can't feel their
light and heat. But the sun is close to Earth.
It gives us the light and heat we need to live.

FUN FACT

People have named 88 constellations in the sky.

Do you see any patterns when you look at the stars? Do you see a bear? A dog? A frog? A fish? The sky is filled with animals.

Long ago, people used the sky like a dot-to-dot game. They connected the stars like dots. They thought the stars were shaped like animals and people. These sky pictures are called constellations.

FUN FACT
You may not always be able to see the Milky Way. It is much easier to see in the country, far away from all the city lights.

18

Galaxies and the Milky Way

There are more stars in space than people on Earth. Like your group of friends and family, stars have groups, too. Groups of stars are called galaxies. Some galaxies have millions of stars. Other galaxies have trillions of stars.

Do you see a cloudy path across the sky? This path is called the Milky Way. It is made up of billions of stars. We live in the Milky Way Galaxy.

So Many Stars

Imagine being a star. You might feel far away in the dark sky, but you would have your galaxy family. Billions of other stars could keep you company.

FUN FACT

All the stars we can see in the sky are a part of our galaxy. If you use a telescope, you can see even more stars. You can also see stars in other galaxies.

Nighttime Dot-to-Dot

What you need:
* a notebook with unlined paper
* star stickers
* a pencil

What you do:
1. Go outside on a clear night, and look up at the stars. Find a group of 10 to 15 bright stars.

2. Put star stickers on a page of your notebook in the same groups as the ones you see in the sky.

3. Find four more shapes, and put them on four more pages of your notebook.

4. Go inside. Connect the stars of each picture with your pencil. Think about the shapes they make. What does each shape look like?

5. Draw in more details to your pictures. You might add hair to an animal or facial features to a person.

6. Get a constellation book from the library. Look at some of the constellations. Compare them to the ones you drew. Did you find any of the same constellations?

Star Stuff

A Long Life

Our sun is between 4.5 and 5 billion years old. People think it will shine for another 5 billion years before it dies.

On the Move

Constellations aren't in the same part of the sky all night. They rise and set, just like the sun.

Holding On

Some objects in space pull on each other. This force is called gravity. Our sun and Earth have gravity. They pull on each other and keep each other close.

North Star

If you live on the top half of Earth, you can see the North Star. It is the only star that does not move all night. Sailors use this star to find their way at sea.

Star Company

Some stars have planets circling around them. The sun has nine planets. People have discovered other stars with planets, too. A star and its planets is called a solar system.

Glossary

constellation—a group of stars that seems to form a pattern or picture

energy—power that makes something go

galaxy—a large group of stars, planets, and other matter, such as dust and gas

gas—something that is not solid or liquid and does not have a definite shape

solar system—a star and the planets that circle around it

supergiants—the largest stars

supernova—an exploding star

To Learn More

At the Library

Mitchell, Melanie. *Stars*. Minneapolis: Lerner Publications, 2004.

Mitton, Jacqueline. *Zoo in the Sky: A Book of Animal Constellations*. Washington, D.C.: National Geographic Society, 1998.Wallace,

Nancy Elizabeth. *The Sun, the Moon, and the Stars: Poems*. Boston: Houghton Mifflin, 2003.

On the Web

FactHound offers a safe, fun way to find Web sites related to this book. All of the sites on FactHound have been researched by our staff. *www.facthound.com*

1. Visit the FactHound home page.
2. Enter a search word related to this book, or type in this special code: 1404811397
3. Click on the FETCH IT button.

Your trusty FactHound will fetch the best Web sites for you!

Index

Look for all of the books in the Amazing Science: Sky Objects series:

Fluffy, Flat, and Wet: A Book About Clouds
Hot and Bright: A Book About the Sun
Night Light: A Book About the Moon
Space Leftovers: A Book About Comets, Asteroids, and Meteoroids
Spinning in Space: A Book About the Planets
Spots of Light: A Book About Stars